The Burning Heart of a Woman
and The Grieving Soul of a Man

The Burning Heart of a Woman and The Grieving Soul of a Man

A Collection of Poems (an anthology)

By

Curtis Wright

Copyright © 2024, Curtis Wright
All rights reserved. Printed in the U.S.A.

No part of this publication may be reproduced or transmitted in any form or by any means, electronic or mechanical, including photocopy, recording or any information storage and retrieval system now known or to be invented, without permission in writing from the publisher, except by a reviewer who wishes to quote brief passages in connection with a review written for inclusion in a magazine, newspaper or broadcast.

Quantity Purchases:
Companies, professional groups, clubs, and other organizations may qualify for special terms when ordering quantities of this title. For information, email info@ebooks2go.net, or call (847) 598-1150 ext. 4141.
www.ebooks2go.net

Published in the United States by eBooks2go, Inc.
1827 Walden Office Square, Suite 260, Schaumburg, IL 60173

ISBN: 978-1-5457-6018-5

Library of Congress Cataloging in Publication

Dedication

To God my creator and savior, thank you for blessing me with this talent. For Irene and Columbus Wright, my parents, I thank you for giving me life. Mom, thank you for being my champion, I love and miss you. To Timekiyo, I thank you for our journey together, I am forever grateful to you. To my children Nya, Matthias and Bethany, you are my world and have made me see things in a new light, daddy loves you all unconditionally and forever. To my biological siblings, Chris, Serina (Ella S. Wright-Scott 1968–1996, I fulfilled my promise), and Cassandra (my twin), I thank you for always being in my corner and allowing me to be me. My Brother from another mother Dr. Bruce Scott Sr. I appreciate all the times we shared on and off the handball court. To my sister friend Stacey Sterling thank you for always telling me the truth and being my support. To my nieces and nephews: Jamel (Jamila & Jackson), Kadeem (Tanika, Serinettee, Trinetee, Kaleb and Felicity) Bruce (Ellianna and Genesis) Christina, and Tionne, you have no idea what your presence has meant to my life. I love each one of you. To one of the dopest artists, I have had the pleasure to ever meet Val Mouzon, The League Center is blessed to have you. Thank you for your sketches, it made my poetry come to life. I look forward to when you publish your work. To Lashay thank you for entering my life when I thought love was all but over and for reminding me who I am. And to all my family and friends, thank you for your prayers, support, honest critiques, and love. You have all been amazing and I am blessed to have you in my life.

Acknowledgments

I would like to acknowledge all those that stood with me. I would like to acknowledge *Leslie Chirchirillo Business Operations Manager and the eBooks2go team for allowing me to fulfill my dream.*

Table of Contents

Dedication — v
Acknowledgments — vii

1. *A Lover's Prayer* — 1
2. *A Song for You* — 3
3. *A Virtuous Man* — 5
4. *Because I Choose* — 8
5. *Black Pride* — 9
6. *Unstable* — 11
7. *Childhood Sweetheart* — 13
8. *Do You Know?* — 14
9. *Don't Cry for Me* — 15
10. *The Most High God* — 17
11. *Escaped* — 19
12. *Always Took for Granted* — 20
13. *From Prince to King* — 21
14. *Give Her, Her Rest* — 24
15. *Guilty* — 28
16. *Have You Ever?* — 29
17. *Heaven Bound* — 31
18. *How Do You?* — 32
19. *I Just Can't Let Go* — 34
20. *I Do Love You* — 35

21. Who Can?	37
22. I Won't Give Up on You	39
23. Will You Miss Me?	40
24. I Wouldn't Let You Fall	41
25. Grateful for Friends	43
26. If I Were to Leave You	44
27. A Soldier for the Lord	45
28. Inside the Heart of a Woman	48
29. Intimacy	51
30. It's Not My Fault	55
31. Laughing...Thinking	56
32. Let Me Be	57
33. Let the Prophet Speak	59
34. Let the Street Say Amen	61
35. Life's Too Short	64
36. Little Africa	65
37. Make Love to Me	66
38. Mama	69
39. Miss Understood	71
40. My Cry in the Dark	73
41. My Daily Prayer	77
42. My Roots	78
43. New Chains	79
44. Nigger Be Free (Part 1)	81
45. Nigger Be Free (Part 2)	82
46. Nigger B Free (Part 3)	83
47. No More	84
48. Not My Child	85
49. On and On and On	86
50. Quintessential Woman	88

51.	*Seduction*	90
52.	*Silent Sam*	92
53.	*When Sisters Talk*	93
54.	*Someone Thought I Was*	94
55.	*Mother to Son*	96
56.	*Son to Mother*	97
57.	*Stop or I Will Shoot*	98
58.	*The Immeasurable Woman*	101
59.	*The Broken Pieces*	104
60.	*The Music in Me*	107
61.	*This Love*	109
62.	*Tonight's the Night*	110
63.	*Twenty-Five*	112
64.	*What a Joy You Are to Me*	113
65.	*What Do You See?*	114
66.	*What I Am Looking For*	116
67.	*What I Am Thinking Of*	117
68.	*Out of Place*	119
69.	*Why I Write*	120
70.	*You and I*	122
71.	*Not Anymore!*	123
72.	*Just by His Grace, I Win*	126
73.	*Did You Know?*	128
74.	*Hey, Brown Skin!*	130
75.	*Hold On (Inspired by Alicia Keys's "Like You'll Never See Me Again")*	132
76.	*Daddy's Little Girl*	134
77.	*My Psalm of Praise*	135
78.	*My Story*	136
79.	*Don't Disturb My Worship*	137

The Burning Heart of a Woman and the Grieving Soul of a Man

80.	*He's Not Him*	139
81.	*The Mask I Wear*	145
82.	*Untitled*	147
83.	*You Are Worth It*	149

A Lover's Prayer

Words can't even begin to form or even express
What you mean to me.
Without you,
For me, there is no next step;
I'm dependent like a baby still nursing,
From the breast, gasping for my next breath.
You were formed and fashioned by God better than the rest;
Even with all your flaws you are still perfect and nothing less:
You're the bone of my bone and the flesh of my flesh.

Your love is like the gentle breeze,
Which blows through the trees,
Seriously arousing each leaf.
You satisfy me,
Shattering the barriers of distance in between
When I reminisce of you and I, my queen—
The two of us make one complete: one mind, one body.

I trust in you and only you no matter whether it's right or wrong,
Because with you is where I belong,
Which keeps me holding on steadfast and strong.
I draw closer to you as time goes on,
And without missing a beat,
You've become the melody to my simple song.

The Burning Heart of a Woman and the Grieving Soul of a Man

The first day I ever saw your face,
Felt your embrace
And screamed out your name,
I cursed the rain
That keeps us apart.
I lie awake at night crying in vain;
Although it's hard to explain.
You are my heart and soul
And when you're hurt I feel your pain.

And I want you to know
I'll keep on loving you,
And all of you
Because you belong to me
And I belong to you.
I can't wait until the day
When I will be tasting you and holding you.
Please keep me in your heart
And we'll be together soon.

A Song for You

I know I don't say it often,
I don't know what's the matter with me.
How can I fix something that's not broken?
Among all that you've given me,
You've sheltered me from the rain.
When everyone else abandoned me,
You know what to say to ease my pain.
All that I am, is all that you've given me.

All that I am, I owe it all to you,
All that I am you made it possible,
All that I am and all that I'll ever be,
All that I am, is all that you've given me.

When I was blind I thought right was wrong,
But you helped me to see,
Deep in my heart, there is a song
And it's all that you've given me.
Because of you, I can fly again;
You've mended my wings
And you've set me free.
You've given me the courage to love again,
All that I am, is all that you've given me.

All that I am, I owe it all to you,
All that I am you made it possible,

The Burning Heart of a Woman and the Grieving Soul of a Man

All that I am and all that I'll ever be,
All that I am, is all that you've given me.

How can I repay a debt of gratitude?
When the most beautiful words just won't do
You've given me life abundantly.
All that you've given,
All that you've given,
All that you've given,
All that you've given me,
Are all that I am.

A Virtuous Man

I saw her from across the street
When suddenly she turned and looked in my direction.
Now, "Was I her selection?" was the question I asked myself.
Although I had seen her many times before,
I was still unsure of what her intentions or motives bore,
Which made her presence hard to ignore.
After a moment, it became obvious to me what she was looking for;
She was looking for a man, but not just any man but a virtuous man.
I then asked myself yet another question:
"Did she even comprehend and understand what it is that makes a virtuous man?
Was it the ring that she saw, which I proudly wore on the fourth digit of my left hand?
Or was it the way she saw me interact and laugh with my better half,
Holding her tightly by the waist
While walking arm in arm to the rhythm of our own pace?
Or could it be that her heart was deceived by what her mind perceived that made her eyes believe in all the wondrous possibilities?"
It could be so because in me she saw all the things in a man she always yearned for,
Even with all the flaws, so she thought.
I watched as she walked toward me wanting me to respond to her stimulus,

The Burning Heart of a Woman and the Grieving Soul of a Man

With the slow licking of her lips and the movement of her hips.
So she leaned over and whispered her name in my ear
And all the things that she wanted us to share...

As I walked closer to him, I felt a little less sober
With each step falling over, feeling less confident than before.
Quickening my pace only caused my knees to shake and my heart to race:
I began rehearsing in my mind all the things I wanted to say
From the first day, I saw him with her:
How he loved her

With his hands and with his eyes,
With his lips and with his smile.
Could he love me the same way and say the same things?
And not love me just between my thighs?
Could he love me despite my heart, soul, and mind?
My body ached, ached to be touched by him.
Engulfed by his flames, I yearned to be his belonging, just to him,
And cherished only by him.
For in him, I saw all the things I needed a man to be:

Both gentle and strong.

So how can this feeling be so wrong?
So with my hands on my hips, I whispered in his ear
My indecent proposal despite my fears.
I was blown away by the words she spoke;
She asked me if I could treat her like a beautiful Black queen,
And do all the things in between and how she had seen me and thought that I was unique

And how she and I could be a perfect fit,
And to my puzzle, she would be the missing piece.
How she could make me happy and be the mother of my child,

And how she could make it all worth my while, I thought of:
If I were to give her the chance, she would be more than just
   my wife,
But also my lover and my friend.
But what she failed to understand was that I could not be her
   virtuous man-
A virtuous man both gentle and strong,

For I am in love with another woman to whom I already belonged.

Because I Choose

I am that once-gifted Black child that most people fear.
I choose not to be silent or bow down to the oppressors' weight
And to shuffle my feet as life comes along.
I speak with a loud voice, showing great intellect and reasoning.
I choose life over death and death over slavery.
I choose not the deprivation and sorrow that destroys the ghetto
With its sickening lazy spirit and quiets the voices of great African
   warriors and thinkers.
I choose not to be a statistic labeled by society as an outcast,
A detriment or a burden.
I choose not to be a crab in a barrel pulled back by my own.
I choose to rise above my surroundings and with a strong Black
Hand and pull my brothers and sisters up with me.
I choose to be a strong Black man supported by his Black woman,
Standing tall and proud.

Black Pride

Whatever happened to Black pride
Had become a far-distant memory
That just faded away and died
With Martin's march and Malcolm's speech.
Did the revolution stop running under Huey's feet?
Give me that Black pride that once united you and I
And made it impossible for our hands and feet to be tied.
Bring back that Black pride my mom and dad once had
Before we were called African Americans,
And just plain old Black.
Bring back that pride that made James Brown
Shout out loud on stage in front of an all-White crowd,
"I'm Black and I'm proud!"
What happened to the real neighborhood cookouts
And block parties in the summertime?
Does it still take a village to raise a young Black child?
Did our pride become replaced by the constant neglect of a society
    that placed us in
Projects as we annihilate ourselves, which reflect the inverse of
    our true intellect?
Nevertheless, we must digress
From the drug dealers in the alleyways,
Piss-stained hallways that rapidly decay our neighborhoods,
Leading our children astray,
And making it impossible for dreams to fly.

The Burning Heart of a Woman and the Grieving Soul of a Man

I long for that same old pride
That stood steadfast and stronger than the American flag:
The one that transformed a young Cassius Clay into Muhammed Ali
Who changed not only his name but also his mentality,
Elevating the conscious state of you and me.
Whatever happened to Black pride,
Started with you and me.
There was a time when mothers raised their children with respect and discipline
And fathers were there to protect and turn their boys into real Black men.
Give me that Black pride!

Unstable

Can't win,
Can't lose,
Because you constantly change the rules.
I won't play the same game;
I simply refuse.
When I'm right
I'm wrong.
When I'm wrong it's worse.
There's no justification
For the pain and the hurt;
I walk through the storm clouds
That you hold over my head,
Constantly playing in my mind,
Realizing the words that you said:
Words like hot liquid
That burns to the soul,
My very soul,
This soul
Has been tattered and torn,
Already too far gone
To see that I was wrong.
Misery loves company.
Is this where I belong?

The Burning Heart of a Woman and the Grieving Soul of a Man

I can't resist,
I won't resist,
I'm tired and weak,
All there for me to do now is just sleep.

Childhood Sweetheart

We started as friends years ago
On a cold winter morning playing in the snow.
You would hold my hand and I would hold yours.
Who would ever think that love is what we were headed for?
As we grew older we grew apart;
We no longer played childhood games and gave someone else
    our hearts.
But one night it was you that I was thinking of;
Then we shared a kiss and instantly fell in love.
I think about all the good times and the laughs that we shared:
Your caress and tender lips when you're not there.
Sweet dreams of you and only you run through my mind.
Someone like you I thought I would never find.
You don't know how much you really mean to me;
I hope you and I will always be
Together forever in love.

Do You Know?

Do you know loneliness?
Do you know how loneliness feels?
Do you know how loneliness seems to come
But never goes?
How lonely I am,
Lonely as...
Or is,
Or was,
In a lonely room
Filled with people
And I'm still lonely.
And I will laugh and dance and cry
And shout and love and sing,
Until I'm no longer lonely.

Don't Cry for Me

My beloved, don't cry for me;
The love I have for you will never cease.
A better place is where I'm going,
Prepared just for me.

Because I have fought the good fight
My reward is nigh.
My name is forever written and
Entered in the lamb's book of life.

So rejoice with me,
For today death has no victory.
Although this body may lie here eternally,
My soul will forever remain free.

For He has placed me underneath His wings
And removed the pain of death's sting.
And He gave me a song of joy and gladness
That only I can sing.

Remember me by the words that I've said
And not by the tears from which over me you've shed.
But remember me for the love that I spread
And also for the life that I have led.

The Burning Heart of a Woman and the Grieving Soul of a Man

So my beloved, don't cry for me;
The time that I shared with you will always be.
I love you all and I bid you peace
Until the day when we shall all meet.

Dedicated to my Sister
Ella S. Wright-Scott June 28, 1996

The Most High God

El Shaddai,
The Most High,
You are the reason why.
Omnipotent,
Omniscient,
Every need is supplied.
Your name,
Your name,
Your name is Great in all the earth,
El Shaddai.
In a barren and forsaken land,
Mannah fell from Your hand.
When the wells run dry,
Well, I
Declare;
El Shaddai
Supplied all my wants and needs,
Supplied my peace,
And supplied every want and need
Abundantly.
I call on You
When I've fallen short.
My gap filler,
Rebuilder,
Intercessor,

The Burning Heart of a Woman and the Grieving Soul of a Man

Way maker,
Change,
Escape,
My last hope;
I sing:
Mighty, mighty
El Shaddai.
He supplies all my needs.
My strong tower,
My dry place in a storm,
My anchor,
All I need,
My sanity,
And my Granted peace,
He is my strength,
Because He is strong.
He is my source.
Cover me
In Your love,
El Shaddai,
Wrap me in,
Hold me in,
I'm safe within.

Escaped

I gazed upon the midnight sky and watched the night turn
   into day.
As the stars and moon began to disappear, I knew the morning
   was on its way.
The night had brought a certain peace that seemed to fill the air.
No violence, bloodshed, or prejudice could be detected anywhere.
I tried to savor every moment, wishing it would only last,
But I knew nothing would be left of that tranquil night and the sun
   was rising fast.
For a moment I couldn't help but feel for a while that I had escaped,
The spiteful nature of every race and most of all their hate.
So I cried and cried as the sun did shine like it does every day.
Then I thought about the other night and for a while, I felt ok,
Because I knew deep down, there will be another time when
   we all will be able to escape.

Always Took for Granted

I always took it for granted
That you'd always be there for me.
I never took advantage
Of the time you had just for me.
I can't understand it,
How you could leave so soon,
But the Master had already planned it.
He knows what's best for you
But still, I cry
From the pain inside.
Your laughter and smile,
I can still hear.
I can't replace
Your warm embrace.
Your smiling face,
Brings me cheer,
And sweet memories of you and me
Forever in my heart,
A better place.
Although we have to part
Forever in my heart;
Forever in my heart, you will be.

From Prince to King

Sitting upon your throne
With those sparkling brown eyes
And those sensuous thighs,
The sun glistens off your caramel tone.
I watched as you glanced from afar, discretely intriguingly
Watching me, Quintessential Queen.
Thinking of you makes thoughts run through my mind,
Which I can't describe with words,
I can't define that which sits upon my tongue like fire.
You and I ought to go to places where we can be alone
And have long, long conversations with
No expectations or limitations of our own.
Then I stop and wonder,
To what degree I would go to love you,
Roll back the tide
Or stop the thunder,
Part the clouds in the sky,
Or tear hell asunder,
For your love;
Yeah, I wonder.
Then would you let me rule your throne?
And wear your crown upon my brow?
Or at least show me how and still allow me to be the man that I am,
Despite the man that I am?
Or would you hold me in your eyes as a helpless child, not a man?

The Burning Heart of a Woman and the Grieving Soul of a Man

Because I am your fairy-tale prince,
Your Hershey's chocolate kiss
And your sweet teddy bear, that fantasy amiss?
I am that smooth melody played on ivory-tickled piano keys.
I am that perfect moonlit night spent on a jet-black beach.
And as you sit upon your throne drawing me close with those
Bedroom eyes, our souls touch before we make love suddenly
I realize that I am holding you close with a touch that was meant to
Do more than just tantalize and with your mind you've got me
Hypnotized.
You see this here, love ain't no one-time thing,
No one-night stand or midsummer fling.
Since my early days of adolescence, I've been destined to be first
And never second my queen,
If you want this prince to be your king..

Get to know me...I already do,

I listened attentively and I heard every word
when you uttered for me to get to know you.
But if you only knew
The things that I already know about you,
Just from watching you,
Then you would realize that I already do know you.
As I gaze into your sparkling brown eyes—
Eyes that embrace like a cool breeze on a hot summer night—
And continuously invite me to stay a while
And not just for a night.
And in the mirrors of your soul, although you try to hide,
I see the burden you carry and the unseen tears you cry out.
And upon your lips I found bliss—
From words that kiss gently,
And simply filling the air with a sweet mist.
In your laughter and smile lie sincerity and warmth

From which relationships are formed:
Bonds that transcend distance and time
That goes on and on and on.
And I do admire and respect
The complex intellect and strength of your mind—
Your thoughts, goals, ambitions, and even the fears you hide.
And I say to myself, "This sister is deep,
But she loves a good time
With fine wine that doesn't pollute the mind,
But arouses the spirit."
Yeah, a good conversation will do that every time.
And I watched as your body moved in perfect motion,
Hair flowing gracefully as you walked with a confidence that most men fear,
And they can't understand
Or they just pretend to comprehend,
But I do understand.
So when I say that I know you, it's from the inside out
And outside in
And not just from the smoothness of your skin.
Because in you I see
One that can move mountains,
Build and destroy great nations.
I see you as the mother of all creation and civilization,
With the courage to love
And with the strength to fall and rise,
Exceeding all expectations
Without limitations,
And never judging falsely,
But always speaking the truth.
And my soul has found solace and contentment
That comes from knowing you.

Give Her, Her Rest

You're a strong Black woman!
But what does that mean?
Does that mean she has to perform?
And live up to society's norms,
Every single day?
Day in and day out?
While being single,
Or singled out for
Her brains and her beauty?
Her strength,
Her acumen
Become her detriments
As more are poured on her than she can hold
Or carry
The load.
As life manages to unfold
Its many ups and downs
Through an assortment
Of disappointments;
She's tired!
Her smile fades
And is gradually replaced.
Through her face, she allows the world to see
The facade.
Although says I am ok

But she is not.
She barely is,
And she still rises
And the very same sentiment is echoed again,
"You're a strong Black woman."
But what does that mean?
Does it mean she doesn't feel?
Or is she impervious to the conditions?
In a condition that she was made to endure,
Not of her own accord.
 She has to always fight, struggle, and battle
To prove her mettle
And not just with strangers
But with the ones that boast and
Claim to lover her most—
 Even the one she calls friend, lover,
Confidant, her shield, and her cover,
As if it were a rite of passage
Or just her turn to
Deal with all the layers upon layers
Of life's stress.
I say,
Give her, her rest
Let her lie down.
Give her, her moment to breathe and exhale
Or just even process.
Give her, her moment on a calm sandy white beach
With the tide gently washing away the sand off her feet.
Give her, her moment of solitude,
Give her, her moment of uninterrupted orgasmic climax
Or however long she wants it to last.
Give her, her moment under the warmth of the sun,
Let the rays bathe her with their brilliance,

The Burning Heart of a Woman and the Grieving Soul of a Man

Sketch by Val Mouzon

Until she has soaked it all in.
Give her what is already earned,
Give her what is due,
Without exception or excuse.
Give her reciprocity,
Give her respect,
But most of all,
Give her, her rest.

Guilty

They put me on the witness stand,
And demanded I tell the truth,
Even though they wouldn't believe a word I had to say.
There was no proof what so ever of me being guilty,
But I knew when the jury would return with their verdict,
That I would be hung,
Because in their eyesight, I had committed the biggest crime ever:
One that didn't have anything to do with the law,
But with the color of my skin.
I was a Black man with a Black face, with a Black name, from
   a Black race, And with a Black heritage, so proud and strong.
So if my being Black offends you,
And I cannot be accepted the way that I am and for who I am,
Then hang me because I am guilty.

Have You Ever?

Have you ever been,
Have you ever been so in love with me
That you found it hard to breathe?
Have you ever been so in love
That your eyes wouldn't allow you to see
Things that weren't a reality?
Have you ever been tempted to throw caution to the wind,
Forget your mind,
And let your heart win?
Have you ever been hurt,
Broken,
Confused,
Because you loved too much
Too hard,
Too soon?
Have you ever been crushed by the very thing that you loved,
To only discover that it wasn't love?
Have you ever made a list of how your love would look
In your mind,
Like the pictures from a book,
Realizing that your fantasy
Was out of reach,
And settling for a little piece?

The Burning Heart of a Woman and the Grieving Soul of a Man

Have you ever desired and longed
For that special place
Where you belonged
And felt love's warm embrace?
Have you ever?

Heaven Bound

It's nights,
Like this, when I'm all alone,
This is when I think of that heavenly place called home.
The stars are out in their space, and the moon is hung in its perfect place.
The sky is a beautiful midnight blue and all the things that I hold true.
I look at how it glistens and shines, hoping that one day, it will be mine.
I watch the birds on how they soar through the air, with a graceful flight done with such care.
With a rainbow to guide me to my life's goal,
My prayers have been answered more than threefold.
When the earth is still like a straight line is when I'll be with my Savior till the end of time.
It's nights,
Like this, when I'm all alone, is when I think of that heavenly place called home.

How Do You?

How do you grow
When you know
You are not
Supposed
To be
In this place?
In a state
Of less and
Living regrets,
Filled with pain and misery,
How do you rise
Against the winds and tides
That constantly
blow like tropical storms,
when deep inside you feel
Those things come alive?
How do you stay and remain
The same when the rain continuously pours
And beats down
Like heavy fists on doors,
Harrowing sounds that haunt
And disturb your very peace,

Curtis Wright

The little peace that you have,
That you seek?
I ask,
How do you grow
How do you?

I Just Can't Let Go

How can something so right be so wrong?
I thought our love could weather any type of storm.
I turned around and you were gone,
So what's the use of holding on
To bittersweet memories of yesterday's song?
I just can't let go.

What am I supposed to do?
Life's not the same without you.
My heart aches and the pain won't be subdued,
When I reminisce about a kiss shared between me and you.
I just can't let go.

I still can't believe that tomorrow will be
Without love, without hope, and without you and me.
Together for all eternity,
This I thought was our destiny.
I can't let go.

I must let go and now I realize it
Through a broken heart and teary eyes.
There are no regrets and no last goodbyes.
We've already spread our wings,
Now, it's time to fly.

I Do Love You

From the first day that I met you,
I saw you and I loved you
Without knowing anything about you.
Beautiful you are by far;
You are everything I want and need,
And by some strange miracle, you walked into my world
And made my life complete.
Anything you ask of me you know I can't deny,
But still, you ask me why.

Among the million things you've given me,
Is the joy you bring to me;
You are my destiny.
A thousand angels could not possibly sing
The sweet song that you sing.
You are my river when my well runs dry,
But still, you ask me why.

I can write a letter that goes on and on forever,
Telling you how much I really love you.
But would that make it any better?
I'd be faithful to you until the end of time,
So, remove all doubts from your mind,
But still, you ask me why.

The Burning Heart of a Woman and the Grieving Soul of a Man

Don't ask me why,
Just know that I do love you.
With an everlasting love
That belongs just to you.
And if you don't know by now,
Then please allow me to show you how;
For with this ring, I do vow.

Who Can?

Who can?
I was ten years old when my dad left.
Or should I say passed?
I say the word *left* as if he were coming back.
I say the word *left* because it feels like he had left.
He's on a long trip and just had not come back yet.
You know one of those trips where they would
Go away for an undisclosed amount of time
And return unexpectantly with something nice as a way of saying sorry for being
Away for so long, hoping that it would make up for the lost time.
The lost time,
The lost time,
It's as if it were just misplaced somewhere else,
On high, or on a shelf where you could reach and pick it back up again,
And would just take it because you were so happy to just see them again.

Yeah, one Friday afternoon, my dad left.
He did not even say goodbye,
Or tell me to take care of the house,
Or even put me in charge or anything like that.
There was no excuse,
Or story.
Why he just left us all with red swollen eyes,

Without being able to even see through eyes that cried rivers
    of tears that cascaded
Uncontrollably down my face?
They would not stop.
Even if I asked them to,
They would not stop flowing,
Because my reality
Had been shattered.
Like the revelation of the tooth fairy and Santa not being real,
He left without teaching me how to shave,
Or how to shake a man's hand and look him in the eye.
He didn't teach me how to fix a flat tire,
How to paint a wall or patch it.
All he left me with was so much knowledge that did not pass on.
That's why, I grieve and mourn.
He left me unprepared for life.
He left me without teaching me how to be a man
For my children and wife.
He left and I can't undo the past
And past transgressions
From unlearned lessons
That rips at my very soul,
My thoughts
And my deeds.
Who can confirm for me?
My identity is incomplete;
It's based on fallacies
And inaccuracies.
From brothers in the barbershops,
On hallowed corners
Signified in the street.
My validity is
Left up to me.
Who can but me?

I Won't Give Up on You

I know it's hard to say
When you've made mistakes
But it's ok.
When you think I should
Because no one else would be
By your side, I still stood.
When times get rough
And you've had enough
Of the hurt and pain you've caused
To the ones that you love,
When you feel you can't go on
And that all your hope is gone and
When you are weak for you, I'll be strong.
With all the things we've been through,
Even if you tell me to,
I won't give up on you.

Will You Miss Me?

I would miss you
And I hope you would miss me too.
As much as life is and such
Spinning
Out of touch
Reality
Not so much
You didn't even miss me
Just my luck.

I Wouldn't Let You Fall

Before I let you fall
I wouldn't let you fall for me so fast,
So deep,
And so intimately.
If I didn't have any intentions of catching you,
Catching you in my arms,
And holding you
Long and tight
With all my might,
I wouldn't let you fall.
If I didn't have any intentions of taking care of you,
Taking care of every want and need,
And supply it before you even speak,
Intercede,
Or whenever you need it,
I wouldn't let you fall.
If I didn't have any intentions of supporting you,
Supporting your dreams,
Supporting those things
That seem out of reach
And help you achieve them,
I wouldn't let you fall.
If I didn't have any intentions of making you smile
While we danced and dined
To a sultry midnight whine,

The Burning Heart of a Woman and the Grieving Soul of a Man

I wouldn't let you fall.
If I didn't have any intentions of catching you

And making you, number one in my life,
My lover, my friend, and my wife,
My beautiful quintessential queen
And I would be your handsome devoted king,
Keeping fears aside
And taking a step
Into your wanting heart,
I wouldn't let you fall.

Grateful for Friends

I'm grateful for friends
That stay until the end
And never hesitate to lend,
Even if it's their last card.
Such a friendship surpasses all,
Even without having to ask.
I'm grateful for friends who manage to touch with
Their hands and their heart,
My hands and my heart,
Regardless of how close or far apart.
I'm grateful for friends with whom I can grow old;
They are the sunshine in my life,
And the laughter in my soul.
I am grateful for friends like you,
Because you have managed to be
All those wonderful things I see and more to me.

If I Were to Leave You

If I were to leave you, what would you do?
Would you journey on toward tomorrow's road
Or stay at a standstill and make some excuse?
If I were to leave you would you weep and cry
Or wish me well with a warm embrace
As we say our last goodbyes?
If I were to leave you would you begin to recollect
Of yesterday's time that was spent?
If I were to leave you, for some day I must,
Be sure to keep faith in tomorrow's trust.
I leave you now although it may be too soon,
I bid thee a farewell and to thee, adieu!

A Soldier for the Lord

I'm a soldier for the Lord;
I've been in many wars,
And fought many battles,
Just for the cause,
But I've never gone into battle
Without my shield and sword,
Got my armor on,
Rugged and steady.
I stay ready;
There's no need for applause,
That's what soldiers do.
With the breastplate of righteousness;
Loins girt about with truth,
Suffered many wounds,
And almost consumed.
He said He will never suffer my foot to be moved,
Battered and bruised,
Broken and empty,
But still, God I choose.
I've been hit in friendly fire that wasn't so friendly,
And wasn't aiming straight.
They thought I was the enemy?
Or were they just pretending to be
On the same team
So they can put an end to me?

The Burning Heart of a Woman and the Grieving Soul of a Man

All the years,
All the tears,
This is what I've been training for,
This is what I've been working for,
This is what I've been praying for,
This is what I've been fasting for.
So, there's no way to avoid this war.
There're so many casualties
Around me needing help,
And trying to intercede
That it left me weak,
Feeling uncertain and unsure,
And insecure
Father please, I cry,
I'm trying to endure
But I'm feeling all the weight
Crushing me down
And pushing me down.
I can't escape it,
I'm prostrate,
Lying flat on the ground.
Even in the face of death,
I cling to the Word with my very last breath,
Reciting scripture after scripture,
Feeling like there's nothing left,
And depressed from the pain and stress.
The pressure is building and building
Until it's too much.
Like Paul, I'm fighting the good fight,
So I can't give up.
With a sword that is drawn,
Let the enemy be warned.
I won't stop until my last breath is gone.

Curtis Wright

It's not until I stop and pause
That I remember the battle is not mine; it's the Lords.
The battle is not mine; it's the Lords.
The battle is not mine; it's the Lords.
I've got sweet victory, sweet victory.
I'm a soldier for the Lord.

Inside the Heart of a Woman

He called me all sorts of derogatory names,
But he still loved on me.
He was ashamed of being with me in public,
But he still loved on me.
He said I was no good,
But he still loved on me.
He said that no man would ever want me,
But he still loved on me.
He laughed at the color of my skin,
But he still loved on me.
He said that I was not his type,
But he still loved on me.
He criticized the shape of my thighs and the sag in my breast,
But he still loved on me.
He talked about the kinks in my hair,
But he still loved on me.
He always complained about the food that I made,
But he still loved on me.
He's never satisfied with the love and sacrifices that I made,
But he still loved on me.
When she put him out,
I still let him love on me.
He loved on me and loved on me and loved on me
Until I was bare.
How could I let him love on me?

Sketch by Val Mouzon

The Burning Heart of a Woman and the Grieving Soul of a Man

Because I had forgotten to love myself,
I had forgotten that my name is beautiful.
I had forgotten my true worth;
The value of my breast, my thighs;
And my mind...kinky hair and all.
I had forgotten about his dreams
That I helped birth into the world.
I had forgotten how I had been his anchor below;
His strong leveled foundation
And his sky above
For him to aspire to reach.
I had forgotten how I had given him the strength—
My strength to climb out of his pit of despair.
And when I had finally remembered,
I then realized
It was his insecurities,
His shallowness,
His imperfections,
And the smallness of his manhood
That he did not want me to see,
But I did see,
And I loved him unconditionally, despite that.
Although he was unworthy of my love,
And he rejected me,
So I no longer let him love on me.

Intimacy

Hey, babe, I'm home!
As if I couldn't smell the strong scent of your cologne
Perforating the room before you entered,
Lingering,
And attempting to be the center of attention.
"I got something for you!"
But do you have what I need?
Beside flattering vain words are
Red-bottom shoes, two sizes too small
That hurt my feet,
Chanel bags,
Dresses by Versace;
All are just material things.
I need intimacy,
I need to be stripped bare,
Stripped bare of not just my clothing,
But every part of me,
Every title,
Every label gives me heartache
And my pain,
My everything.
Lay me down gently,
Instead of foreplay,
Just ask me about my day
And listen

The Burning Heart of a Woman and the Grieving Soul of a Man

Sketch by Val Mouzon

Intently,
Not just with your ears
But with your eyes and heart as well.
Can't you tell that I need intimacy?
I need the most intimate part of me to be filled,
Penetrating more deeper,
Still a depth,
Unmeasured, but felt
I need continual intimacy,
Not intermittently to satisfy my soul.
I need more than just your hands,
I need you to be into me,
Attuned to my mind and soul
And not just my body.
Massage away fears
That come to evoke
And make me feel less than who I am
Because I am
And I am all
Wrapped up in this tiny ball
Of energy.
I need more,
I need intimacy.
So I scream it,
Dream it,
And crave it.
You see,
It allows me to be
The woman I am.
I don't need fantasies.
I sit in my reality,
Understand it,
Demand for it,

The Burning Heart of a Woman and the Grieving Soul of a Man

From a man that is not afraid
To undress me and see
All my vulnerabilities,
And still love me.
I need intimacy
And in return,
I will give you a throne,
A place of your own
From which kings and queens are grown.
All of me,
Nothing is better than reciprocity
As long as you give me intimacy.

It's Not My Fault

It's not my fault,
I am this way,
Born a Black man in supposedly a minority race,
And living in what you call a ghetto
Where drugs and death are an everyday part of life,
Just trying to survive and find peace of mind.

It's not my fault when you hate me because of the color of
    my skin, or because of some misconception you have heard
    about me, or because I respond differently to your stimulus.

I cannot apologize, nor do I wish to apologize for who I am
    or what I am.
I am Black, strong, and proud and God says that I am beautiful.
    It's not my fault.

Laughing...Thinking

Laughing out loud and thinking silently, we crossed that road, allowing fate to take its course. I couldn't believe that I could feel so close to someone in so short a time.

It was as if we once flew the same skies sometimes crisscrossing each other's path,
And allowing just enough time for us to steal a moment that would last a lifetime.

Laughing out loud and thinking silently, we rode the tides to shore
And then walked hand in hand on a freshly combed beach,
Leaving behind only our footsteps to remain as a symbol of the time that was spent.

Laughing out loud and thinking silently, we climbed the highest mountains,
And never once looked back and regretted the struggle that we shared,
And all the time looking for more mountains to climb.

Laughing out loud and thinking silently, two worlds collided, becoming one
And sharing each other's dreams and ambitions.
And together we faced all obstacles and climbed all mountains all the while laughing out loud.

Let Me Be

Let the earth stand still beneath my feet which move swiftly
   towards you.
With every step you take, I take upon the unproven ground,
Leaving behind footprints in the sands of time.
Let these two feet be supported by two strong legs in which
   to be your
Anchor planted firmly amid winds and storm:
With a muscular wide back that cannot be broken and made
   to bend at the waist
Always moving forward and never allowing your back
   to be pushed up against the wall:
Followed by strong broad shoulders made for you to lean on
And to lay the weight of your world upon mine,
Attached to immense sculpted arms with the strength to reach
   all the way down and lift you out
Of your troubles and carry you through,
Holding you ever so softly but tight in the middle of the night.
At the end of those arms, let there be two strong hands with
   the power to
Destroy and move mountains and with the skill to build you
   a castle.
And I'll hold your dreams safely in the palm of those same hands.
Along with a thick massive chest, you can lay your weary head
Upon when you're tired and long for rest.
Upon my face, you'll find ears that not only listen but also
   understand you.

The Burning Heart of a Woman and the Grieving Soul of a Man

I have eyes that see your pain and sorrow as well as your beauty
Beholding you in your entire splendor.
I have lips that speak with great confidence and authority
　removing all doubts,
Calming all fears, bringing comfort to your soul with its
Soothing song of peace,
I am held together with a mind showing great intellect
And reasoning being able to resolve most conflicts,
And impart unto you the wisdom to grow and flourish,
Which is ruled by my heart, which I give freely to you.
Let my flesh be encased by a hardened thick exterior singed to
　a golden
Bronze being able to withstand the fiery darts that may cross
　your path.
And I pray to God to let me be all these things to you,
Never wavering without ceasing when you need me to be.

Let the Prophet Speak

I heard this prophet speak the other day,
And the things he said just blew my mind away.
Now, this brother didn't sit in a pulpit
Wearing a long black robe trying to look immaculate,
Spitting that same old feel-good rhetoric
That you hear Sunday after Sunday after Sunday.
This particular message was different than the norm;
It was broken down on Nineteenth Street and Broadway in poetic form
Where a few of us listened intensely to what the brother had to say.
Did y'all see that brother? "Yeah," one sister slyly said,
Admiring the beauty of the dread, but everything he said went right past her head
Because she could see his outer beauty, which is only skin deep, and not see the inner beauty
From the bread in which to us he fed.
Did y'all hear that brother?
"Man, has he finished?"
I always miss it!
I only caught a few words in the last sentence, but it sounded hot.
"You mad props, keep writing!" one brother shouted out.
If he was in tuned spiritually with the energy as he professed,
To be acknowledging the 360 degrees,
Then he would have caught the essence of the lesson with just one sentence.

Did y'all feel that brother?
"Well actually, I was feeling shorty from across the street.
I noticed she was looking at me and I had to go get that number
 you see," said another brother.
As the prophet left, I dropped my head and asked myself,
 "Did you hear, feel, and see him?
Did his words of wisdom invoke a change in my mentality?"
I was not discouraged because of the selected few he had reached.
So, I yelled out loud as he walked through the crowd, "Give him
 room!
Give him room!
Let the prophet speak."

Let the Street Say Amen

There were little brown boys, running down the street
And playing their favorite childhood games to the rhythm of their own beat.
They were innocent and naïve,
Trying to avoid the heat of the summer,
Escaping the madness of another bloodshed night.
There's soul music drowned out by the fistfights,
Alcohol-clouded minds,
Drug deals gone wrong,
Dope fiends try to score,
And fill their veins,
And empty their soul,
Young bodies sold
On the corner at twelve years old little brown boys running down the street,
Trying to avoid urine and feces.
Those bodies stretched out and overdosed bowels relieved.
There was late-night hustle,
And corrupt police
Trying to muscle and learn young.
The path they see
Is a crooked one
With loaded guns,
Fast cars, and faster women,
All after those

And million-dollar bank accounts.
Failed to count the time spent
In the pen,
Doing a five to ten incarcerated,
Emasculated and violated,
And subjugated to jailhouse laws
Made by immoral men.
When broken,
Present dire consequence paroled and early release
Returned back to the same old streets
With new faces only to repeat
The same mistakes
Recycled back to the penitentiary.
Little brown boys were running down the street.
They hear,
They learn
And they see how these streets speak and testify

Of homicides,
Shattered lives
Strategies,
And dreams going awry.
These streets also testify of lives cut short,
Long-fought drawn-out cases in court,
And litigants unfairly represented,
Living in broken-down tenements.
These streets also testify of young adolescents lost in innocence.

These streets testify to all sorts of pains
And some issues too excruciating to name,
Domestic violence,
Violence practiced upon a people
Not taught to see or value themselves as equal.
These streets testify to shame,

Pure and unmitigated claimed
From generation to generation
Where little brown boys play.
They hear people speak
And seek change,
Better days and nights
Filled with tranquility and peace.
They hear people speak and prophesy of future upward movement
Initiated by a movement of a people,
And voices all screaming.
These streets testify of unity and solidarity.
Let us be our brother's keepers
And our sister's teachers
With fidelity,
Struggles and progress
With regularity,
Imparting right from wrong,
Policing our own,
Taking back the village
And no longer divided
But together strong.
These streets will testify
Of no more killing
And perpetrated violence.
And these streets testify and say amen.

Life's Too Short

There is no time to hesitate,
Nor is there time for careless mistakes.
Beware of day dreaming and letting your mind wander.
There is little time to think and ponder.
Life's too short.

Time is ours to spend but not ours to give.
We must make do with the lives that we live.
Be happy but not content.
For life, one day must sadly end.

With laughter and sorrow hope to see tomorrow.
Don't take too long to stop and smell the flowers.
Find something worthwhile to pass the hour.
Life is too short.

Little Africa

Little Africa,
Little Africa,
Can you hear your mother calling you
From overseas in a distant land, I never abandoned you?
Little Africa,
Little Africa,
Be careful of America's deceit.
She will try to make you change your name and destroy your love for me.
So stand up strong, little Africa, like little Ireland and little Italy.
I named you little Africa because you are a part of me.

Make Love to Me

Lie down beside me on soft satin sheets
And with the palm of your hands caress the smoothness
    of my face
Gently planting wet kisses on the indentation of my cheek,
Which causes my mind to begin to fantasize.
Begin to allure me and seduce me with your eyes.
Lay your soft full ample moist lips upon mine
And let your tongue discover its treasure
As it begins to intertwine with mine.
With the warmness of your mouth, you engulf me;
Draw my earlobe into you with sensual small bites
Slightly arousing me.
Make love to me.

Then allow your fingers to roam aimlessly
From the hairs of my chest down to my
Waist and slide into my boxer briefs.
Feel the coarseness of my pubic hairs as you
Undress and fondle me
And I stiffen from the cool breeze.
Make love to me.

Then grab my manhood expeditiously
Placing droplets of ointment on my flesh
And begin to massage me vigorously,
Satisfying your longing desire to taste me in your mouth

And losing all your inhibitions.
I'm raptured in ecstasy from the tight chasm you formed about
    my bow
With grace and precision:
Ready to perform acts of fellatio and cunnilingus
As you straddle me in a sixty-nine position.
Make love to me.

Spread eagle, pin me beneath your weight
As you lay prostrate.
My nostrils become filled with the sweet fragrance that emits
    from you.
While resting upon my face.
Taking a firm grip on my shaft about the base,
Proceed to deep throat me
Until I begin to pulsate.
From your methodical long erotic licks, you placed about my sac,
I shudder under your manipulative touch.
I then commence to explode in an uncontrollable climax.
Make love to me.

Mounting me boldly,
Letting me feel the force and strength of your thighs,
Let your body grip my muscle
As you greet me with your hot-honeyed wetness swelling deep
    inside.
Interlocking our hands
As your pelvis grinds slowly,
Thrusting in an upward motion
Let your hips gyrate uncontrollably.
With each stroke becoming more rapid and intense,
Arching your back takes me deeper inside
At unbelievable pleasure,
I begin to moan and wince

The Burning Heart of a Woman and the Grieving Soul of a Man

With your succulent breasts dangling before me like ripened fruit
    on a tree.
You pull my head in between and make me suck vigorously.
Make love to me.

With a final massive thrust,
I start to erupt.
My toes curled,
Making my body contract and convulse,
Holding me tightly as I lose all control of my speech.
Let me cum inside of you releasing my seed.
Spent and fatigued, you rest your body on top of me.
Make love to me.

Mama

Oxtails, collard greens, candied yams, and black-eyed peas,
Mama would always cook for my brother, sisters, daddy, and me.
Some soul food fixed for six, stretched from three.
Mama would wait until our bellies were full before she would eat.
And for desert, I would watch from scratch as she would make
Some peach cobbler, banana pudding, or chocolate cake.
Licking the spoon was always worth the wait.
With a smile and a kiss on my cheek, she would ask me about my day.
Mama would fix our tattered old ripped faded jeans.
When Dad was mad on our behalf, she would intervene.
She was not there just to keep the house tidy and clean:
But our every-hour problem solver;
She's the most intelligent Black beautiful queen.
She stands only five-feet-two in height,
But a giant in her own right.
Mama knew how to keep the peace when we'd fuss and fight.
She helped us say our prayers and tuck us into bed at night
And with a hug and "I love you," she would say good night.

The Burning Heart of a Woman and the Grieving Soul of a Man

Sketch by Val Mouzon

Miss Understood

My dear sister, let me dispel this myth that all Black men are no good
When it seems obvious to me that you may have just misunderstood
The way that we walk and talk with our style all our own
With perfect African features that are strong and Black to the bone.
Short hair, kinky, nappy, curly, bald, or with long dreadlocks,
Always on our game, smart and clever like a fox,
And we know a good woman when we see one, and we'll let you know, and we'll let you know
And we'll let you know all night long,
Holding you so gently but tight in our masculine arms,
Buy you flowers and candy call you our honey, sweetie, and boo.
These are just some of the ways we express ourselves to you.
We wake you up in the morning with a passionate kiss that is soft and wet
Gazing longingly into your pretty brown eyes, all the while feeding you breakfast in bed,
Place rose petals in your bubble bath, baby oil, the room filled with sweet burning incense,
Rub your back and shoulders when you are tired and tensed
And make love to your mind.
We know when you are angry and read between the lines,
Brighten your day with just one smile

The Burning Heart of a Woman and the Grieving Soul of a Man

And help raise and support our beautiful Black child.
So the next time some sister comes telling you that all Black men are no good,
You tell her, "I'm sorry, Sister, but I think you may have just Miss Understood."

My Cry in the Dark

Sister, I cry!
Sister, can you hear my call?
Can you hear my call?
Sister, my sister!
Let the winds blow from the east, south, west, and north.
Come forth,
Meet me under the sycamore tree
Where we can find shade for our souls
From the sun's sweltering heat.

I heed your call and I respond,
I greet you with my voice,
My energy, and my heart,
As we celebrate our unbreakable bond.
I greet you, my sister, I greet you,
I greet you with warm,
Open arms.
I greet you with dance and song.
I greet you in our native tongue
From which our blood flows.

I welcome your presence
And chant karibu.
My sister, my sister, my sister,
Let nothing divide or come between us.
Opposition may try to impose on us

The Burning Heart of a Woman and the Grieving Soul of a Man

Sketch by Val Mouzon

Sketch by Val Mouzon

The Burning Heart of a Woman and the Grieving Soul of a Man

But whatever betide,
I stand firmly by your side.

For we stand in unison
With our sisters before us
And our sisters to come
And with our sisters present,
We stand as one
In innumerable sizes,
Hues and tones
Beautifully designed
And formed
Uniquely,
We decree,
Umoja,
Unity,
Nguvu
Power
Usawa
Equality
Ujarsiri
Courage
Maelewano
Harmony
And to you, I bid thee peace
Ninakupa amani
Ninakupa amani.

My Daily Prayer

Hide my eyes oh Lord from the things my heart may want
And desire and cannot have:
But give me the wisdom that I might see with clarity the things
Meant for me to find.
Keep my hands from reaching out to those that don't reach back
And to arms that don't extend,
And to remember to reach out to those that do.
Let the ground that I walk on be solid and firm.
Stop my feet from walking toward paths that weren't meant for
Me to tread upon.
And if I fall and my life surrendered, keep oh Lord my soul intact
And make me dwell therein.

My Roots

My roots run deep into the earth, which anchors me and my tree,
A solid foundation withstanding time and storm.
They will live forever,
My roots are strong.

New Chains

Quickly like a mighty hawk, closing in on its prey ready to devour,
Overcome, and over power its weak and helpless victims, they came
Binding our hands and feet as I knew they would.
They bring with them chains for us to carry, which wasn't necessary but because they could, they did.

Now with the chains of old gone, a new plan of slavery was calculated.
Self-enslavement is what it is called when we are the captors of
Ourselves and it's our mind that is involved:
We are impressed not depressed,
Yes, because on our forefathers' graves, we swore to them our very best.
How sad it is to see a race of people by their own hands annihilated, God forbid!

It's been hundreds of years of backbreaking work from picking
Cotton to tilling the earth.
From once great African kings and queens derived common drugs and
Alcohol fiends destroying the lives of both young and old.
To see with my eyes the loss of one's pride,
I could no longer hide the shame and anger I felt inside, so I hid.

With every fight for freedom comes a new name,
A new face of someone that can stir up the soul and emotion

The Burning Heart of a Woman and the Grieving Soul of a Man

Of a fallen race, whether it is Nat Turner, Sojourner Truth, or Martin Luther King
Motivating, liberating, and paying the highest cost
To let freedom reign.
We press on,
We move on,
We keep fighting the good fight knowing that one day we will break
The chains of yesterday, today, and forever be free of that old slave mentality,
And that's the reason why we live.

Nigger Be Free (Part 1)

This is no way for a Black child to be.
Nigger be free, nigger be free.
Born into the hand of slavery,
Nigger be free, nigger be free.
Born into a life of misery,
Nigger be free, nigger be free.
Born to be whipped and hung on a tree,
Nigger be free, nigger be free.
Born because my master raped me,
Nigger be free, nigger be free.
Born and stripped of your name and history,
Nigger be free, nigger be free.
In your death is the only peace for you I see,
Nigger be free, nigger be free.
Lord, I'm asking You to help me please,
Nigger be free, nigger be free.
I've taken the life of my poor child and set him free,
Nigger be free, nigger be free.
It was the only way that nigger would be free,
Nigger be free, nigger be free.
I saved his poor soul and I wished that nigger be me.
Nigger be free, nigger be free.

Nigger Be Free (Part 2)

I was born in the land of slavery,
Nigger be free, nigger be free.
Now I will be 103,
Nigger be free, nigger be free.
I worked in the field till I was 93,
Nigger be free, nigger be free.
My family is gone and now it's just me,
Nigger be free, nigger be free.
My last wife died when I was 73,
Nigger be free, nigger be free.
My body is crippled and I cannot see,
Nigger be free, nigger be free.
And on my deathbed, my master came to me,
Nigger be free, nigger be free.
He said, "You're not dead yet you're still my property,"
Nigger be free, nigger be free.
So I closed my eyes and went to sleep,
Nigger be free, nigger be free.
Yes, Lord, let this nigger finally be free!

Nigger B Free (Part 3)

My great-great grandfather's name was Nigger B. Free,
Nigger be free, nigger be free.
But he was born in the years of slavery,
Nigger be free, nigger be free.
He didn't live to see our people set free,
Nigger be free, nigger be free.
He died on a plantation at his master's feet,
Nigger be free, nigger be free.
He didn't get to see us gain our civil peace,
Nigger be free, nigger be free.
Nigger be free,
And become a negro,
A colored man,
A poor free Black,
An Afro American
And after that,
No more plantation fields
And cotton bale,
Nigger be free to spend his life in jail.

No More

No more to give to you my love,
Our love is at an end.
No more to give to you my love,
My patience is wearing thin.
My love, my love,
Your tender touch I will sorely miss you.
Your so ever-soft shapely breasts and the sweetness of your lips,
I tried to give you all my love
But I simply have had enough.

Not My Child

As I walked down the street I could see the pain in her eyes.
"I'm homeless could you help me," was her only cry.
Tattered garments draped off her fragile frame,
The cold air ripped through her body
With her hands stretched out for the world to see her shame and need.
All she could do is beg and plead,
But "Not my child," was the reply.

He stood in the corner arms folded right over left not even old enough to understand the concept.
Pulling on a joint, "This is the bomb," he said.
Baggy pants sagging off of his waist, hat turned back, "I'm all that."
His feet draped in the latest gear.
Only thirteen years old, his heart was so cold to the flow of cash that passed through his hands
So blind that he never saw the bullets that struck him down.
At the funeral, I sat and cried but you didn't and I asked why, and you said, "Not my child."

Worthless old drunk, snotty-nosed punk, crack head, drug dealer, pimp,
Whore, hooker, felon convict, prostitute:
If not my child or your child, then who is to blame, heroin or cocaine?
Then whose child is it that life passes by every day?
Then whose child is it that society lets fall by the wayside?
How long is it before it is yours and mine?

On and On and On

I say I got to go,
You understand the circumstance.
Let's leave our plans for romance till another day,
Then you smile trying to hide the pain inside
But the foolish pride you can't deny it's written on your face.
"Honey stay, I'm all alone don't you leave.
Can't you see deep inside, it's all a lie and it's really killing me?"

I've been there before you wanted more.
The warning signs went out the door, and I'm sure I can't ignore the obvious fact,
That you're leaving me.
It's crossed my mind a thousand times that love ain't blind.
It's not surprising,
I can't believe I'm on the verge of losing you.

I finally found that peace within
Can't let this end my lover friend,
So, why pretend the way I feel?
Now tell me what I am supposed to do;
I'll make a change.
Let's rearrange.
This situation can't remain.
If you're not there, then it's all in vain.
I need you here with me.

I'm missing you, you're missing me.
If love's the key, then I'll wait for my turn for you and me.
What's got to be has got to be is not my style.
So, tell me,
Are you the one for me?
This goes on and on and on, on and on and on.
The words to my song...

Quintessential Woman

Oh, what a perfect and beautiful creation you are, a rare marvel
    to be seen,
Captivating and exuberating all the attributes of a queen.
Prominent philosophers and noblemen all flock to hear you speak,
Even the great Nefertiti would bow in your presence humbly
    at your feet.
So strong is your back, the back that bears the burdens of men's
    souls.
Compare you to another I do not dare do to you,
Because in you, I see the finest treasures of jaspers, rubies, and gold.
A goddess bearing the sweet nectar of many a rose,
There is no pedestal, nor is there any title too high for thee.
The Quintessential Woman is what you are to me,
The Quintessential Woman may you be for all eternity.

Curtis Wright

Sketch by Val Mouzon

Seduction

It started oh so innocently
Between you and me,
With meaningless everyday conversation,
Promptly arousing in me a fascination,
Which quickly changed into infatuation.
Was it the long engrossed eye gaze
Or was it circuitous or the sideways way
That now and then allowed me to steal glances
And waiting for the opportune chance?
Or was it the long silence shared
In close spaces creating an intimate scene?
Your words become effervescence,
I'm captivated by the language you speak eloquently,
Dropping me to my knees
And reduced to not being used to
Or wanting to
Display my feelings of vulnerability
Which somehow crept up on me.
You've seduced me
First with your mind
And then by the curvature of your spine,
Wishing to elongate the time
I fantasize
About the swell of your lips
From a perfectly placed kiss

On sacred places
Where you'd restrict
Your mahogany skin
Spread thin
Like the skin prostrated over the head of the drum
Producing a deep pitch
When struck and played with my forefinger and thumb.
You are my muse,
Inspiring me to the heights of a greater interlude,
And momentary interruption of protection
As I satisfy my unquenchable thirst diminished by
Animalistic lust from forceful thrust,
From the passion that exudes
And from a touch that lingers
Long after you have come and gone,
Promptly quieting my volcanic eruption.
You are my sublime seduction.

Silent Sam

Whoever said that silence is golden,
Never heard Silent Sam speak
With his eyes or smile or
With every gesture that he makes.
Living in his own world of loud thoughts
And silent words, life for Sam seemed to be so simple,
But yet so cruel and
I, too, wished to be like Sam:
He was happy and content.
You could never see his tears or hear his cries,
But you'd cry for him.
In a far distant corner sat Silent Sam
Without a worry or a care in the world—
A world of silent prayers, silent love, thoughts, and silent dreams.
I cried and cried for Sam to speak,
But he never uttered a word,
He just simply waved and smiled.

When Sisters Talk

When sisters talk they smile and laugh,
They listen attentively to each other's words and body language.
When sisters talk, they groove to their own rhythm
And vibe to their own beat.
When sisters talk,
It's from the heart
And connects to each other's spirits,
Even if they are miles away.
When sisters talk,
They steal back the time that was lost,
And make new memories
That can never be erased.
As sisters do, which you both have done,
You are truly sisters indeed.

Someone Thought I Was

Someone thought I was beautiful enough to love,
Special enough to keep,
And loved me anyway,
All the way deep,
Unashamed of me,
And all of my insecurities.
Someone loved me
And not just privately
Or whenever convenient
But made me an essential priority.
Someone thought I was precious enough to share,
And include me in their dreams and ambitions.
All made clear
Their intentions,
Future certain,
It was their plan.
Someone thought I was worth investing in
All their time,
All their energy was
Invested in me spiritually and emotionally.
Someone noticed and was able to see
Things in me,
Which I didn't believe
Turned my fantasies into reality
All because someone loved me.

Curtis Wright

Sketch by Val Mouzon

Mother to Son

By Langston Hughes
Well, son, I'll tell you:
Life for me ain't been no crystal stair.
It's had tacks in it,
And splinters,
And boards torn up,
And places with no carpet on the floor—
Bare.
But all the time
I'se been a-climbin' on,
And reachin' landin's,
And turnin' corners,
And sometimes goin' in the dark
Where there ain't been no light.
So boy, don't you turn back.
Don't you set down on the steps
'Cause you finds it's kinder hard.
Don't you fall now—
For I'se still goin', honey,
I'se still climbin',
And life for me ain't been no crystal stair.

Son to Mother

I know life for you ain't been no crystal stair.
I've seen some of those steps you climbed and wondered how.
So, I started climbing those same steps;
Some two at a time.
I felt good and strong.
So, I shouted out loud quite arrogantly, "These steps aren't so hard."
Then I looked up and I saw you, fixing those same torn boards,
And smoothing out those same old steps that you climbed before me,
Leaving behind a clear path for me to walk on,
And then I smiled because I no longer wondered how,

I just knew why
It was for me you kept climbing all those stairs.
It was for me you didn't turn back.
So Mama, don't you worry none,
I'm still climbing too,
And when you get tired, just look over your shoulder;

There, I'll be cheering you on.
I know life for you ain't been no crystal stair, but you always made life easier for this here Black child.

Stop or I Will Shoot

Stop or I will shoot,
Hands up,
Face down!
But they still shoot,
Unload and then reload,
Cutting Black bodies into two,
With their Glock issued
15 mag
Had a weapon
Wouldn't comply
Looked menacing
Is the excuse
Now we are being shot
In parking lots and
Through the windows of our own homes
For leaving our doors open
With one wellness phone call
Should have known
Wrong apartment Black man was shot dead
Like Black Panther Fred Hampton
40 years ago was murdered while sleeping in his bed
With the Barbeque Beckys
Calling the law
On Black innocence
On the pretense of

So-called breaking the law.
My fear is for every Black adolescent
And yet they yell the slogan,
"Let's Make America Great Again."
When has it ever been
For me and him?
Those with brown and dark skin
Guess they never heard of the 400 years of slavery
Followed by Black codes,
Midnight riders
Ku Klux Klan
Jim Crow,
The system of leased convicts,
Which to this day still exists.
They must have forgotten about Rosewood
Tulsa's Black Wall Street.
The Devil's Punchbowl
In Natchez, Mississippi,
The marching
The civil rights
Dogs and hoses
Places reserved for only Whites,
The separations,
Segregations,
King's, Malcolm's, and Medgar's assassinations,
The flooding of drugs into the inner city,
And wrongful incarceration.
Now getting back to the subject at hand,
Let me see your hands
Is the given command
Before the man
Is pumped with bullet after bullet
Without fear of repercussion,

The Burning Heart of a Woman and the Grieving Soul of a Man

Indictment,
Or judgment.
Stop or I'll shoot!
So what am I to do?
Flashing before my eyes
I feel like my life is over.
Even if I comply,
My son and daughters are watching,
And afraid.
Not wanting their daddy to die,
They say he was a good man,
Worked for the school,
Positive role model,
Teacher of the Year too,
But none of that matters now as I take my last breath.
Just another unarmed Black man shot to death,
I never thought it could happen to me.
So many others must have thought the same thing.
Stop or I'll shoot
Everything is gone in an instant;
Next time it might be you.

The Immeasurable Woman

Most things are measured by
And given value and
Treasured by,
But then devalued
But how do you measure
The immeasurable woman?
How do you measure her tenacious spirit,
Her courage, her strength
And her endless capacity to love?
By depth or by length?
How do you measure the kindness in her eyes?
The softness of her smile,
The intellect of her mind,
Intrinsic value,
Goes undefined.
How do you measure the passion of her speech?
The comfort of her arms,
The inestimable lessons that she teaches,
And her precious gems she freely gives and shares
From the once adorned crown, she wears.
Indentations are the only indications
That the jewels were once there.
How do you measure her beauty?
By color or by race?

The Burning Heart of a Woman and the Grieving Soul of a Man

Sketch by Val Mouzon

Do you measure her apparel?
Or the size of her waist?
Do you measure her talk,
Her walk,
Perfectly clothed in grace?
How do you measure the immeasurable?
It's a mystery to me.
The immeasurable woman you are.
Let all the world see
How immeasurable you are
With no limit to your worth.
The immeasurable woman,
Immeasurable at birth.

The Broken Pieces

The broken pieces,
Do they belong to you?
I found them
Lying there
In the corner,
Scattered.
Was it from him?
Was he the cause?
I saw them
Lying there,
Like hidden gems
Shattered.
All that remained
Were the little shards;
Those precious pieces
Left for someone to sweep away and discard
Like useless trash
But they aren't
Still lying there.
He left behind
Pieces of a whole
Broken beyond,
And unable to repair;
So he hoped and thought.

Sketch by Val Mouzon

The Burning Heart of a Woman and the Grieving Soul of a Man

I carefully picked them up and carried them from over there.
I know you didn't want me to see them
For fear and insecurities.
No, I won't stare
Or do I even care about
The broken pieces?
The very part of you,
The broken pieces,
That left you scarred and bruised,
I love every part of you,
Even the broken pieces,
Especially the broken pieces,
Those broken pieces.

The Music in Me

A whopping bop be bop secondly do bam, a razz a ma taz.
Hear the sounds of that old big band.
Hear the machine-gun sound of the snare drum pound.
The sweet melody of those ivory-tickled piano keys
Played to an up-tempo beat.
Feel the groove and move off that bass-line scale
As the blare of the horn and snap of the fingers fill the air.
Daddy O, out of sight, man that cat's crazy
The sound of that old big band goes the music in me.

Chink splat klank, chink splat klank goes the sound of heavy chains
All rhythmically and methodically moving the same way
Binding Black skin to his and her kin,
Binding Black skin to the will of other men
Feel the crack of the whip across the back of another African
   brother, rebelling
Against the hands that oppress people of color,
Running fast, running strong, running on, planning their way of
   escape through
Negro spiritual songs.
Woe oh woe, woe oh woe, the music in me goes on.

There's a loud cry of their voice and the stomp of their feet;
Hear those African drums tell a story with every beat.
With thunder, they dance, and with thunder, they do chant with
   great strength

The Burning Heart of a Woman and the Grieving Soul of a Man

And unity.
And with wisdom, their tribal elders speak, with their pupils
    listening attentively at their feet.
They walk with great pride, dignity, and with their heads held high
"We are great warriors," is the call echoed to you and me,
We are great warriors proud and free,
We are great warriors, goes the music in me.

This Love

This love of yours, this love of mine;
This love is brighter than any sunshine.
This love is pure, this love is real,
This Black love has its own sex appeal.
This love can't wait to taste your strawberry lips; to your smooth and creamy thighs;

To your oh sexy hips.
This way, that way, whichever way it turns,
This love feels so good when you let it burn.
So then I stop and open my eyes, and dab the sweat from your brow.
Baby, because when we will be making love, it's not just to pass the hour,
This love is blind, this love is strong,
This love can do no wrong,
This love knows no boundaries, this love knows no limit,
This love cannot be bought, because this love is a gift,
This love is so big that it conquers all.

But yet it lays perfectly inside you and me, oh so small.
This love comes in all sorts of sizes, shades, and colors,
This love was made especially for lovers.
There's brown sugar, golden honey, redbone, caramel, and my favorite chocolate,
So come and get yourself a scoop, if you think you can handle it.

Tonight's the Night

Tonight's the night, my brothers and sisters
That we dine alone.
We kick the devil out from amongst our tables.
No longer will he be able to eat and grow
Strong while others grow weak.
He will no longer be allowed to dip his hand
Into the bowl where we eat from
And pollute the sustenance that we use to
Nourish our bodies with his lies and deceit.
We will not allow the table scraps to fall
Carelessly to the ground for his
Consumption and if any happens to fall to
The ground,
We will step on his neck
And snatch that very crumb from his mouth.
And after we kicked him out from our
Table and out of our house, then we will
Kick him out of our community by pulling
Our brothers and sisters, sons
And daughters, off of the streets.
We will disrobe them of the filth and
The negativity that corrupts and destroys the
Lives of our youth and then clean them up
And dress them with dignity, self-respect,
And pride.

Curtis Wright

We then need to pull our mothers and fathers
Out of the allies and the bars and show
Them that they are the reason for a sliding
Generation but now is the time for the sliding to stop.
We will then throw our arms around them with
Love and kindness and heal the wounds of
Not only the young and old generations
But all generations and generations to come.
And when that devil is finally defeated
And driven back to the hells from whence
He belongs, then we will be able to rejoice
And rebuild our once a great nation.
So I implore you, my brothers and sisters,
Let it start here and let it start now. Tonight's the night.

Twenty-Five

It's not every day that a Black man gets to see age twenty-five.
I feel blessed to be alive.
I walk around with my head held high.
I reach beyond the heavens so I can touch the sky.
Twenty-five, twenty-five.
Not twenty-five kids with twenty-five wives.
Not twenty-five to life:
But it, sure enough, feels like.
You see, ever since the day I was born,
I've had dreams that were stepped on.
I've been lied to, and cheated on,
Talked about, ridiculed, and so on and so on.
You see, I'm at the end of my rope and I got to hold on steadfast.
Will I last as time goes past?
Trying to exist is like a fish out of water.

If you can't breathe, then you ought to know
That life ain't no crystal stair,
Ain't no good times here,
Only when the family is there to
Protect you, help you, correct you:
Then can you even expect to rise above the ghetto-
Ghetto life, ghetto codes, ghetto minds, and ghetto roads.
At twenty-five, I'm alive.

What a Joy You Are to Me

Heaven rained down on me with tears of joy
And I could not even see
The day you came into this world.
You made my life complete.
With your smiling face, you've astounded me
As I held you safely in my arms,
And you cast a spell of love that surrounded me
As you overwhelmed me with your charm.
With your weeping eyes, I beheld you
And with a heart that was filled with such pride,
You can depend on me to comfort you,
Whenever you start to cry.
There is nothing I won't do for you;
My little girl is what you will forever be,
And I just want to let you know
What a joy you are to me.

What Do You See?

They say this is a night about expressing ourselves
Well,
Here I am,
I mean, here I am.
Look at me, sir, ma'am,
Tell me, what do you see?
Do you see a poor Black child living in poverty?
Do you see my anger and hostility?
Do you see a gang member or a thief?
Or that familiar drug dealer out on the streets?
Or do you see vivid dreams?
Of the next generation of kings and great thinkers,
Motivators and speakers,
And world changers and teachers.
The truth is that they all want to be us
All I am asking you is, how do you see us?
Anything less,
Then you will never be able to reach us
Because if you don't see us as something more,
Then we will never be;
So, blame it on yourself
Before you blame it all on me
Because together we can change the perception
Of how we are viewed.

Curtis Wright

We can change the projection
And our future too.
But it all starts with how you see me
And how you see us.
So look beyond my shame,
Look beyond my clothes,
Look beyond the labels used.
To change my rightful name
Look beyond all the stereotypical
Characterizations of me
Because I won't let the media with all its lies
Define me.
So, tell me, what do you see?
I see an intelligent young Black man,
Gifted and strong,
Standing before me.
What do you see?
Intentional,
Innovative,
Inclusive,
Every child, every day.

What I Am Looking For

What I'm looking for
Is someone I can adore,
Give my heart, my soul, and my life to,
My everything and more.
Someone that I can trust
And trust me to love,
Exclusively unconditionally;
That is what I'm thinking of,
Someone that makes me smile
When I look into her eyes.
I laugh for no apparent reason.
The feelings I just can't hide
What I'm looking for is someone that will trust me to love
Unconditionally and exclusively.
That's what I'm thinking of.

What I Am Thinking Of

I am thinking of a soft passionate kiss
Upon your lips
Or below your hips.
Whichever mood it fits
Makes my body stiff
With anticipation:
Which makes up for all the waiting
While conversating
About all the things we find fascinating.
And nothing fascinates me more
Than being able to explore
Your mountains, valleys, seas, and shores:
Being careful not to ignore
Your most erogenous zone,
And your body blown
Tender kisses placed here and there make you subtly moan
Until you scream out my name,
Which only intensifies the pain.
Free falling for your love
While I taste your candy rain
And you make me want to do
All the things you want me to
And so much more because I'm into you.
You make time stand still with your sex appeal
As you lay down beside me.

The Burning Heart of a Woman and the Grieving Soul of a Man

Now how does that feel?
But I'm not finished yet,
Not until
I've at least repeated steps 1 and 16
And all the ones in between.
Then I climax with my very last breath,
Wiping the sweat
From the very depths of your orifice
Midnight missed.
Now isn't this bliss?
And to think that it all started with the thought of one kiss.

Out of Place

When I'm out of place,
Out of Your will,
Far from grace,
Your love never abases.
It draws me near,
Washes over,
And covers me,
Gently,
and rescues me,
When I'm fallen.
I hear Your voice
Call out my name.
I can't believe
In my misery;
In my tumultuous time,
You lift me up
And won't let me stay
In these feelings of condemnation
And of shame.
You've broken every chain;
How much You love me.
It's above me
To think or conceive
Or imagine it.
A love like this could never exist.

Why I Write

People sometimes ask me why I write.
Like I
Need a reason,
So I try to explain
Through paper and pen
And complex thought.
And when
I begin to
Jot,
I write and ignite
The fire in me and in others,
So they can see the flame,
That burns and scorches
Like torches
Lit directly from the combustion of the sun
Piercing my soul,
Because I'm a writer
Fighting to write
Because this is my life.
I write for the truth.
I write to
Right those wrongs.
But most importantly,
I write for you,
The youths,

So you can tell future generations to come
Why do we riot and won't keep quiet about
Breanna Taylor
And George Floyd,
Why Colin took a knee
The senseless death of Ahmad Aubrey,
So you can write about Black excellence
And our exploits,
And not how we were exploited
By those for whom the wrong ones intentionally voted
Because skin folk ain't always kin folk
Which has been duly noted,
You can write our story,
And your story,
How you see it
And how you live it,
Your voice,
Your choice
You can shape the world
To how you see fit
Like an army standing strong.
Your might is your pen.
That and your mind,
Is your only weapon needed.
You can defeat any foe
If you believe it.
This is why I write,
This is who I will be.
I write to you.
Will you write to me?

You and I

Together
We can
Touch the sky.
It has always been
You and I.
Through the storm,
We will survive.
I can't tell you
How much it means to me
To have you right here,
Always knowing
You are by my side.
Just you and I,
Together and forever
We can fly,
And also make impossible dreams come alive.
Just you and I.

Not Anymore!

You've been walking in and out
Of the door,
Back and forth,
Leaving our babies-
The ones we made.
There's no child support,
You can't even support yourself,
That's why you're back again,
But this time,
I'm not letting you in.
I'm not going back
To the same old lie
That you've changed.
This time's going to be different.
Why?
Just because you say
So now, I am supposed to be ok
With the way
You just abandoned me,
Abandoned us,
And left us
With broken dreams
And broken trust.
I'm not going back to the hurt and the deceit,

The Burning Heart of a Woman and the Grieving Soul of a Man

To the children crying,
Whenever you leave,
And then you return,
Wanting a hot plate,
Respect for your name,
Like your loving is great,
But I've moved on
Like the song.
I've grown strong
Because I know my worth.
I don't wish you any harm.
Just leave me and mine alone
So a real man can step in
And not one that just pretends to be a man,
But the one that can stand
In times of good and bad
And I will stand with him.
I will stand beside him,
I will stand behind him,
And remind him
Who he is and his greatness.
And if one doesn't happen to come,
I will still be ok.
But you coming into the house,
Is not today.
I have children to raise
And raise them above the constant
Nonsense
That prevents families from staying together.
Generations of brokenness
Have become the norm-
The walking in and out.

Curtis Wright

I can do without
The back and forth,
And in and out the door
From you;
Not anymore.

Just by His Grace, I Win

With a gasping breath
And the fear of death
All around me,
My mind was distraught,
Filled with wrought,
Anguish and pain.
Shalom has found me
Wrapped me in His arms,
In His Love,
In His Strength,
And in His Wings.
He's my everything,
Jirah,
And Provider.
Even when I've gone astray,
In the wrong way,
In the thickets of the woods
Filled with thorns,
Lost in my sins
And thoughts,
I can call on Yahweh
And He will save
Me,
And rescue me
From my brokenness,

And my emptiness
That causes bitterness
To overflow
In my misery.
But El Roi,
He's the God that sees me.
Jehovah Rapha,
The God that heals me
Completely.
On the cross,
His Love was revealed
Unconditionally.
He is a strong tower
And a mighty shield.
I find grace
To take me through
Another day.
I find grace,
The grace that He has given me
To stand strong in Him
And all His might,
The grace He has given me
To win the fight
Because His will is right.
With a gasping breath
I win the fight,
I win.
I win!

Did You Know?

Did you know you could fly?
Did you know?
I saw you tuck in your wings
When both feet left the ground,
Preventing the wind from lifting you up
And then you returned safely
Not wanting to take flight.
Even though you were compelled to
You didn't think I saw it
But I did
And just like that it happened again,
But this time you stayed off the ground even longer
And you flew higher
And higher.
Did you know you could soar so high?
I mean really high.
Like you belonged
All along.
You didn't know how good the warmth of the sun would feel on your back.
You didn't know how the weight of the world would just disappear
With every care
Enjoying the journey
And every now and then
Swooping down low enough

Just low enough to
Steal a moment
Before returning to the skies
And you flew
And you flew
And you flew
Like I knew you could.

Hey, Brown Skin!

Have I told you how beautiful you are
Even with your so-called flaws
That make you withdraw
When you look in the mirror?
But I say how unique you are:
With your uneven smile and your pouty lips
Made especially for me to kiss.
I can't even possibly pretend
Not to stare every now and then
In awe at your beautiful brown skin.
I get so aroused when I think about all the intimate things
The love songs we sing
And the love that we make—
With my hands placed firmly about your waist
From the back with your hair pushed back—
With every stroke matching the rhythm of your pace.
I like the touch of your smooth and soft brown skin on mine,
Your legs wrapped around mine—
Holding you tightly with a passionate embrace
Your fingers running down the small of my spine.
I love the taste of your succulent brown skin
Especially when I'm playing with your taut round nipples
Between forefinger and thumb
Biting each one gingerly

As I let them dance around the tip of my tongue.
So I then start to lick
Down to the curves of your hips
Stimulating your clit,
Your juices flowing like hot molasses sweet and thick,
So I sip until I had my fill
From night until
And as you lay peacefully resting next to me
I watch you silently.
I can't resist awakening you with a good morning kiss
And I say, "Hey, Brown Skin."
You know your so-called flaws
That make you withdraw
Well, I see nothing but perfection
And how beautiful you are.

Hold On (Inspired by Alicia Keys's "Like You'll Never See Me Again")

Are you ready?
We are going for a little ride
Inside my heart and mind.
Steady now
Steady
I can't sleep at night
Without you by my side.
When I close my eyes
I see every moment spent together
I see all the tears I've cried
The ones meant for you and I.
Lord please, Lord take away
This pain I feel,
Feels like when Heaven's gone
This is how you make me feel
Never ever be another
No one quite like no other
That can ever take the place of you.
This emptiness
That exists
Is all because of you
And I pray

God will make a way
For you to stay
Here
'Cause you take my breath away
With your very essence
Just to feel your touch
Is like a present to me.
Your love is enough
To fill me up
Don't want you to ever leave
Stay!
Stay!
Stay!
Stay with me always.

Daddy's Little Girl

When you opened up your eyes
Heaven smiled down on you
I'll always be there by your side
When no one else is there for you.
I'll hold your hand when you take your first step
Then pretty soon you'll begin to take two.
You brought me so much joy with your first breath
It's like a dream come true.
And through the years
I've watched how you've grown
We've shed many a tear,
And now you have a family of your own.
And although at times I may seem so far away
And you feel all alone and so afraid
Just remember one thing is always true
That you are daddy's little girl
And daddy loves you.

My Psalm of Praise

When I'm out of place
Out of your will
Far from grace
Your love never abases
It draws me near
Washes over me
Gently
Rescues me
When I'm fallen
I hear your voice
Call out my name
I can't believe
In my misery
My tumultuous time
You lift me up
And won't let me stay
In these feelings of condemnation
And shame
You've broken every chain
How much you love me
It's above me
To think or conceive
Or imagine it
A love like this exists

My Story

They don't know
They don't know the story of me
Only the glory they see
Of what my father had decreed
Throughout the heavens in the earth
Over my life come to pass
Despite my past
Disobedience
My sin
My fall
Wondering if I will ever rise again
To see your face
Stand in your presence
Abandoned in my own shame
Condemnation has taken His place
Fleeing from His grace
Distant
For I have forgotten what the author has written
Concerning me
My destiny lies within Him
My victory is sure and sweet
They don't know the story of me

Don't Disturb My Worship

I stood in line
Waiting so patiently
For my time
For me to see
Your Face
Your Glory.
Chains are broken
Off of me
My shackles are gone
Here's my chance
I can freely dance
Before my King,
And I will sing
Hallelujah
To the one
True and Living God
My offering
Alone I bring
I didn't come for a show
No form or fashion
I present my gift
So don't disturb my worship.
Don't bother me
When my hands go up
And I bow before the King

The Burning Heart of a Woman and the Grieving Soul of a Man

Don't disturb my worship
Don't bother me
When I cry my Savior
My God You have delivered me
Don't disturb my worship.
Don't bother me
As I give way
To give you all the Glory and Praise
I lay prostrate
At his feet
Don't disturb my worship.
Don't bother me
When I'm in His presence
I find rest in.
Don't disturb my worship
Don't bother me
Join in and enter in
So you too can be free.

He's Not Him

I can't help but remind myself every time I see him
That he's not him
And when he enters the room
It changes my energy, my mood
Significantly
Putting me in a place
Where I just need space
To socially distance myself
So that I can breathe and exhale
Contemplate the decision I made
To commit my mind, my body, and my soul to him
But he's not him.
And although he's been good to me
I mean really, really good to me
Better than most
He just doesn't fulfill my needs
Where it matters the most
When I look at his eyes, his lips, his face,
They don't hold my gaze
His words don't hold my attention
I don't feel that euphoria
My heart doesn't race
Or pound excessively
Uncontrollably.
I don't feel that connection

The Burning Heart of a Woman and the Grieving Soul of a Man

Sketch by Val Mouzon

He doesn't penetrate my mind
With revelations
Because he is not him.
And now here he is approaching me
Wanting me
Desiring me
And I want to give in
But he's not him
I've tried to replicate him
In all the ways that mattered most
Gave him purpose and an identity
Using the perfect constructs to mold him
And to help him grow
Despite all my efforts and intentions
He had not the drive nor the ambition
He's not him.
Taking off my clothes
He lays me gently on the bed
Caressing me
Kissing me tenderly
But he's not him
So, I close my eyes and pretend.
I let his hands roam aimlessly
His tongue moving in and out
Feeling my body begin to stiffen
My hips lifting
Up to meet his
Pulling him deeper inside of me
And I imagine it is him
My legs wrapped around the small of his waist
Squeezing my thighs until they ache
Feeling a swell from deep within
Until I explode

The Burning Heart of a Woman and the Grieving Soul of a Man

And yell
"YOU'RE NOT HIM"!
Wait,
Did I say that out loud?
I think he may have heard me…
My head starts to spin
"I'm not him,"
Come again?
Well, that's what I heard
My worst fears realized
But I'm not at all surprised
As her hands touched my face
Looking into my watery eyes
Finding a hurt she could not undo
And with all her might she held onto me
Forcibly with her arms and legs
My body numb
After all these years
I poured into her
Worshipped her
Built her up
While falling down
Let her lead
While I followed
Let her dream
While I swallowed
The bitter herb
Of unfulfilled
That left me exposed
With gaping holes,
Wounds that could not be
Stitched, bandaged, or closed
Left me weak

And vulnerable to all the
Cruelties and harshness the world had to offer,
Which I readily accepted
Because it was her, I wanted to protect
But I'm not him?
My heart betrayed
No longer wanting to stay
As hurt began to be replaced by anger
A rage I wanted to express and unleash
As those words replayed in my head again
And, again
"You're not him."
All these years
I was just a substitute
For you to use
And abuse
My emotions and feelings
Have me reeling
When I think of
The time wasted
The wasted time
Wasted years
Wasted tears
The lies told
Of forever,
Which I was willing to share
And he left you at a moment's whim
But I'm not him.
And I refuse to silence my voice
To be her second choice
And allow this to continue anymore
No more words left to be said
Tears shed

The Burning Heart of a Woman and the Grieving Soul of a Man

Releasing her from our vows
And the sanctity of our marital bed
So she would no longer have to settle for less
Less of
Less than
No longer needing to pretend
I'm not him
I'm better than him.

The Mask I Wear

I am tired of wearing this mask
I am tired of pretending
So, don't ask
If you really don't want to know how I am feeling
I'm trying to go through this healing
Process
That has gotten me
Seeing things clairvoyantly
That I've never seen
Or refused to see because of this mask
That I wear
But I bared
My own burdens
So that you might share
Your love
Your life
Your gift with me
So I wore it all these years
Uncomfortably
So that you may be
And through silent tears
I shed
I gave my all
Not knowing it was never enough
To keep us wed

The Burning Heart of a Woman and the Grieving Soul of a Man

So I remove the mask
Letting go of all the pain
The anxiety
The fear and pressure
That arise in me
The feeling of failure and
Insecurity
So how I'm feeling
You no longer have to ask
Just look at my face
I've removed the mask.

Untitled

I walked down the hallway thinking I heard your voice,
    your laughter.
Wanting to feel your energy.
Forgotten what it had felt like.
To see your warm smile
Taken for granted, you would always be here.
Now silence fills the place where there once was.
Now there are only memories...

The Burning Heart of a Woman and the Grieving Soul of a Man

Sketch by Val Mouzon

You Are Worth It

It's never been easy for me to say
I love you
They go unheard
Simple words
With all things I've been through
I've been left for dead
Many tears I shed
Battered and bruised
But I will try again
Again, and again
To rise up again
Just for you
Because you are worth it
You are everything to me
Because you're worth it
You make my life complete
Because you are worth it
Know that you're worth it
I would travel back in time
Just to find you all over again
Just to see your smile
It's worth the while
That I'll ever get
And then I pretend

The Burning Heart of a Woman and the Grieving Soul of a Man

Sketch by Val Mouzon

Like 50 dates
Like it's the first time we ever met
Because you are worth it
You are everything to me
Because you're worth it
You make my life complete
Because you are worth it
Know that you're worth it
You can have everything.
That life may bring
I'll give you the sun and the stars
And I will take the clouds
The rain
Your darkest days
Your wounds and your scars
All of your hurt and your pain
I willingly bear
And hold them close to my heart
Because you are worth it
You are everything to me
Because you're worth it
You make my life complete
Because you are worth it
Know that you're worth it
And if by circumstance
Or unlucky chance
I had to leave you here today
I thank God for the guiding light
That led you my way
There are no regrets
With my dying breath
I faintly whisper,
"I'm so in love with you"

The Burning Heart of a Woman and the Grieving Soul of a Man

As I close my eyes
For the very last time
You are still worth it
And I hope you think
I was worth it too.

www.ingramcontent.com/pod-product-compliance
Lightning Source LLC
Chambersburg PA
CBHW070103080526
44586CB00013B/1169